I0140920

THE ART
OF
SACRIFICE

Anthony Clarvoe

BROADWAY PLAY PUBLISHING INC
New York
www.broadwayplaypublishing.com
info@broadwayplaypublishing.com

THE ART OF SACRIFICE
© Copyright 2005 by Anthony Clarvoe

First printing: November 2005
I S B N: 978-0-88145-293-8

Book design: Marie Donovan
Word processing: Microsoft Word
Typographic controls: Ventura Publisher
Typeface: Palatino
Printed and bound in the U S A

THE ART OF SACRIFICE was written with the support of a Playwrights Horizons/Amblin Commission. Its writing was assisted by readings by Playwrights Horizons, Primary Stages, 78th Street Theatre Lab, and Merrimack Repertory Theater.

The world premiere of THE ART OF SACRIFICE was presented by Merrimack Repertory Theater (Charles Towers, Artistic Director) on 13 November 2005. The cast and creative contributors were:

WILL ....Nesbitt Blaisdell
ARON ....Jeremiah Wiggins

Director ....Charles Towers
Set .... David Evans Morris
Lights .... Juliet Chia
Costumes .... Jane Alois Stein
Sound .... Jamie Whoolery
Props ....Michaela Duffy
Stage managers ...... Emily McMullen, Adam Scarano

NOTE

This edition of THE ART OF SACRIFICE has been published to coincide with the premiere production, and does not include any revisions made during the rehearsal process.

ACKNOWLEDGMENTS

In addition to the collaborators listed above, my thanks to the following for their work on the readings that helped bring THE ART OF SACRIFICE to fruition:

Playwrights Horizons: Tim Sanford, Lisa Timmel, David Esbjornson, Harris Yulin, and Ben Schenkman. Primary Stages: Casey Childs, Andrew Leynse, Elliot Fox, Tyler Marchant, George Grizzard, and Michael Stuhlbarg. 78th Street Theater Lab: Eric and Ruth Nightengale, Ethan McSweeny, Brian Murray, and James Ludwig. Merrimack Repertory Theater: Charles Towers, Harriet Bass, Jack Davidson, and Harry Carnahan.

My gratitude to Jamie Horton and Doug Harmsen for my first hearing; Kip Gould for this book and much more; John Golbach, my chess buddy; the late Frank A Clarvoe, Jr for teaching me the game; Sam Clarvoe for asking me to teach it to him; and Kate Clarvoe for love and talent, an inspiring victory, and many, many sacrifices.

CHARACTERS & SETTING

ARON, *thirties. An international grandmaster*
WILL, *sixties.* ARON's *father*

WILL's *living/trophy room*

Time: the present

The beauty of a game of chess is usually assessed according to the sacrifices it contains.
Rudolph Spielmann, *The Art of Sacrifice in Chess*

Sacrifices only prove that somebody has blundered.
Savielly Tartakower

The way to refute a sacrifice is to accept it.
Wilhelm Steinitz

Scene One

(WILL's *living room. Functionally furnished.*)

(*On every available wall space, floor to ceiling, even in front of the window, hang the kind of inexpensive open shelves that you can buy at the hardware store. The shelves are filled with trophies, loving cups, plaques, ribbons, framed citations, certificates, clippings, and photographs. The trophies range from the few that are shining and fresh to the greater number which are coated in darkening shades of tarnish and dust.*)

(*Night*)

(ARON *is dressed for travel, with a dark coat over what from the fit and condition looks to be a good but second-hand suit. He has put down a battered briefcase that would hold a notebook computer.*)

(WILL *is dressed for bed, in a faded robe and pajamas.*)

(ARON *carries a grocery bag out of which peeks a large and ornate trophy.*)

(*They move, oblivious to each other.*)

WILL: Something wakes me up. He's standing at the door.

ARON: I drive up. No. I'm driven to the door. From—

WILL: He'll say—

ARON: The bus station. No, train station. Airport. Yes.

WILL: And I'll say—

ARON: I walk in.

WILL: And I'll say, what I meant.

ARON: I'm wearing...like when I was a kid. No.

WILL: All I meant.

ARON: No, I'll wear the suit. He'll like the suit.

WILL: No, first I have to...

ARON: I'll carry the trophy.

WILL: I'll invite him in.

ARON: In a box? In a bag?

WILL: Do I hug him? Shake his hand?

ARON: In my hand.

WILL: Nod?

ARON: *(Nodding)* Yes. *(He takes the trophy out of the bag.)*

WILL: He kisses me on the cheek like when he was three years old. Before everything.

ARON: Nothing will be different.

WILL: Everything will be just like he remembers it.

ARON: But he'll see how I've changed. He has to.

WILL: He'll be his old self again.

ARON: I'll stand there.

WILL: He'll relax.

ARON: No matter how tired and hungry I am.

WILL: He'll make himself at home.

ARON: I won't sit down right away.

WILL: Don't get pissed off again. Don't.

ARON: I'm going to get there in the middle of the night.

WILL: *(Suddenly shouting)* What were you doing? Why did you do that?

ARON: He'll open the door, and as soon as I'm inside he'll turn his back and go. Knowing I'll follow him. By the time I do, he'll be sitting in that room. His generation, they always put the king in the corner too soon.

WILL: And if I said...

ARON: And then he'll say...what?

WILL: So who died?

(They look at each other for the first time.)

WILL: Quite the suit.

ARON: This is how I dress now. Didn't know if you'd be up.

WILL: I don't sleep much anymore.

ARON: You never slept much.

(Both are aware of the trophy. Neither acknowledges it.)

WILL: You haven't taken some money job, have you?

ARON: No.

WILL: The suit. You had me worried.

(They watch each other.)

WILL: Why aren't you at the Nationals?

ARON: I am at the Nationals.

WILL: What happened? They haven't posted today's results.

ARON: They're probably still playing.

WILL: Wait a minute.

ARON: It's fine.

WILL: Why aren't you playing? You didn't lose, did you?

ARON: No.

WILL: You did, you lost, you've lost, Jesus Christ,
I don't see you since God knows when, and this is
why you show up?

ARON: No. I had a rest day coming, I asked to take it
early.

WILL: Why?

ARON: I told them I had a family emergency.

WILL: What family emergency?

ARON: Well, my father thought I lost and he fell down
dead.

WILL: That's not funny.

ARON: It's a little funny.

WILL: No, because you're trying to make jokes.
You only do that when you're worried.

(They watch each other.)

WILL: Do they know where you are? The tournament
people?

ARON: They send their best.

WILL: They hate my guts. You told them you were
coming to see me? I bet that put fear in their hearts.

ARON: I bet it did.

(Beat)

WILL: *(Nodding to the trophy)* So that's from last year?

ARON: Which? *(Looking at the trophy in his hand)* Huh!
What have we here?

WILL: Come on, come on—

ARON: Oh, this?

WILL: What have you got for me?

ARON: You want this?

WILL: Give it here, give it here.

(ARON *hands over the trophy.* WILL *sets it in his lap and dandles it like a grandchild.*)

WILL: Hello, shiny guy! Look at you! (*To* ARON*)* It's beautiful.

ARON: Got your eyes.

WILL: You made me wait long enough! (*To the trophy*) Oh, I've been thinking about you. You are even bigger than I expected. So much bigger than the last one.

ARON: The prize funds get smaller, the trophies get bigger.

WILL: It's gorgeous. Welcome! Come meet the family! I've been saving a special place for you. Right here. (*Setting the trophy in an empty spot on a shelf, rearranging some of the older trophies*) Everybody bunch up a bit. Make room, make room. That looks great, doesn't it?

ARON: Sure.

WILL: (*Taking down the trophy again*) Oh, but I've got to hold onto you for a while before you go to bed. Shiny guy, this makes my year, seeing you.

ARON: So, Dad. Hally called me.

WILL: Really.

ARON: About the last time you guys talked?

(WILL *is silent.*)

ARON: He was really upset. He paged me in the middle of the Nationals.

WILL: He paged you at the Nationals, he broke your focus to tell you that we talked on the phone? He calls me every week. What possessed him?

ARON: He said you weren't making any sense.

WILL: I have never made sense to Hally.

ARON: He said you were incoherent. You told him you were coming unglued.

WILL: Unglued? Unglued. Like I was glued before? And now I'm not, and that's a bad thing?

ARON: Then he said the line went dead. And he couldn't get through to you again.

WILL: I don't know what that's about.

ARON: I didn't know what I was going to find here.

(They watch each other.)

WILL: So when you face the unknown, this is what you wear?

ARON: I thought I might have to make funeral arrangements.

WILL: This is what you're going to wear to my funeral?

ARON: No, this is what I want to be buried in, I'm showing you 'cause you're going to outlast us all.

WILL: God forbid. So you want to call Hally, tell him false alarm?

ARON: I'll wait a little.

WILL: I'm fine.

ARON: Till I figure out what's going on.

WILL: Nothing's going on. False alarm.

ARON: Dad. Please. Move One, you scare Hally, and you know, Move Two, he's going to call me, and I'm not going to dismiss his feelings, what with everything, so Move Three, I'm going to do what he wants, drop what I'm doing and come here. It's a three-move sequence, a tactical shot. So what are you up to?

(Beat)

WILL: You guys were worried. I'm... That's touching.

ARON: Call him.

WILL: Me? No, I'm incoherent. Let him stew.

ARON: You are, to this day, such an asshole.

WILL: Secret of our success. So you've reconciled, you and your brother. That's great.

ARON: We get along fine. Always did.

WILL: Always did? He hated you.

ARON: Oh, I know.

WILL: Hated your guts.

ARON: We got along. Is there anything to eat?

WILL: That depends.

ARON: Oh, could we not? I'm hungry, I've been traveling all day.

WILL: You want to eat?

ARON: Yes, Dad, I want to eat.

WILL: Have you done what you need to do?

ARON: As a matter of fact, can I tie up the phone line later, I need to go to the websites, work on tomorrow's game.

WILL: Do it now.

ARON: It'll keep, I'll work better with a little blood sugar.

WILL: What did I always teach you?

ARON: You always taught me the strongest person wins. May I please have some food?

WILL: Help yourself.

ARON: You know what? It's your house. When you want to offer me something to eat, I'll eat.

WILL: Up to you.

ARON: Dad. Why did you say that to Hally? That you'd come unglued?

WILL: I did not say I'd come unglued. I might have said I'd been feeling like I'd gotten a little unstuck. Not unglued. Unstuck.

ARON: I don't know what that means.

WILL: I don't either. I just remember saying it.

ARON: He said you were shouting it at him.

WILL: And that was my last call with him? They mush together, those calls, they're all the same, your grandson this, your granddaughter that, the milestones rolling by on a very flat landscape.

ARON: They are very nice children.

WILL: They are boring children.

ARON: No.

WILL: They are not champions.

ARON: No.

WILL: They will never be champions at this rate. Of anything.

ARON: Hally sounds like they are sweet, funny little people.

WILL: Eh.

ARON: God, you're awful. That man calls you every Sunday.

WILL: Like clockwork. But you! You're back!

ARON: Just for the night.

WILL: No, no, no, I mean you're number one again.
The new magazine came, did you see it? Announcing
the Nationals. There you are, on the cover again. The
Defending Champion. Where is that, I was showing it
to Doctor Rubinstein—the way they wrote about you!
Swashbuckling, they said.

ARON: Swashbuckling?

WILL: Something like that. Cutting a swath, that was it,
the defending champion cut a wide and deadly swath
through the field last year. Did you do that?

ARON: Wide and deadly.

WILL: Recalling his youth, they said. His fabled youth.
Was it fun winning it again after all these years? All on
your own?

ARON: Yeah.

WILL: The champion of the United States. The spacious
skies, the amber waves of grain. You're champion of
that.

ARON: Yeah.

WILL: The fruited plain.

ARON: What are you up to?

WILL: God shed his grace on thee. I'm being nice.

ARON: The fruited plain?

WILL: Well, I started hearing myself. But I meant the
other stuff. Is it fun? You get recognized?

ARON: At tournaments, sure, people know me. There
are times—I was walking through the terminal here—
God, it's stupid, walking along, thinking, I am the
champion chess player of the United States! Make way!
Make way for your champion!

WILL: That's how you should be thinking. The purple mountains' majesty. You're champion of that.

ARON: Yeah, right, shut up.

WILL: Did you see—the magazine, there was a piece about that kid, the one who came up about when you did, what was his name, real little nightmare for you.

ARON: Nick? Joel? John?

WILL: John.

ARON: What's he done now, playing in Europe or something?

WILL: He's retired!

ARON: He what?

WILL: Another one down!

ARON: He's retired? John's—what's he going to do?

WILL: Some money job. Executive assistant to some big financier or something.

ARON: John. Jesus.

WILL: Don't get grief-stricken, what's wrong with you?

ARON: Thirty years, a couple of times a year I have to play against John. And he's just gone? He was almost the only one I learned something from when we played.

WILL: You beat him in the final at the Nationals last year.

ARON: His clock ran out.

WILL: You beat him, I watched the moves online.

ARON: I could have beat him, I was a pawn up in a minor-piece endgame, but I didn't want to blunder, so I sat back and let him lose on time.

WILL: Good gamesmanship.

ARON: It's not my favorite way to win, it's like watching a man drown, frantic little futile...I can't get stronger if everyone who can beat me quits the game.

WILL: Aron. If everyone who can beat you quits the game, you don't need to get stronger. You'll be the best one left.

ARON: That's not the point.

WILL: Yeah. It is. Only a quitter would leave the game for a money job.

ARON: You had a money job.

WILL: I had to have a money job, I had kids to feed.

ARON: So do they, some of them.

WILL: They have kids? Chess people? Big mistake.

ARON: I'm sure.

WILL: Big, big mistake.

ARON: Heard you the first time, Dad. I take back what I said, I have got to get something to eat. *(He crosses away.)*

WILL: Hey! Where're the big guns playing this week?

ARON: Dad.

WILL: I know, I know, I'm sorry, it's just great to have somebody to talk chess with. Are they in Linares?

(ARON stops.)

ARON: Yeah.

WILL: Strong field this year?

ARON: Strongest ever, say the ratings.

WILL: The ratings are messed up.

ARON: Yeah.

WILL: You should be over there.

ARON: I wasn't invited.

WILL: You should be, you're strong enough. It's an
unfair system. Hey, but who's this new kid?

ARON: Hally didn't mention you were manic, Dad—

WILL: I've been seeing online, this new kid, from
Kazakhstan, Uzbekistan, someplace, he's thirteen
or something, stomping everybody?

ARON: He's a novelty, you know how it is. We've been
there.

WILL: Thirteen-year-olds are outranking you and you
want to eat.

ARON: Well. Not so much now.

WILL: Good. Work, it'll give you an appetite.

ARON: I'll eat while I'm online. You want anything?

WILL: You think that kid from Uzbekistan eats before
he works?

ARON: Oh, God damn it.

WILL: Well?

ARON: Dad. I cut a wide and deadly swath.

WILL: A year ago.

ARON: I'm the champion of the United States.

WILL: I hate to see you wasting your time.

ARON: Then why am I here with you?

WILL: Because you need a kick in the ass! Like you
always did!

ARON: And here I thought it was because Doctor
Rubinstein, in addition to congratulating me on
the cover of the magazine, told me you were sleep-
deprived and starving to death.

(They watch each other.)

WILL: You've been talking to my doctor?

ARON: You've been stalking me online. Now.
Do you want anything from the kitchen?

(Beat)

WILL: There's not too much in the kitchen. I need to shop.

ARON: There's nothing at all in the kitchen, is there.

WILL: I need to shop.

ARON: God damn it, Dad.

WILL: I am not starving. Do I look like I'm starving?

ARON: Malnutrition, that's what it means.

WILL: So you and Hally're thinking, what? Old man's going gaga?

ARON: No, that is not what I think.

WILL: And you're here to judge me? To judge if I'm competent to take care of myself? You?

ARON: We wanted to be sure you were okay.

WILL: And you figure you're a fit judge of that?

ARON: Dad. Heard you the first time. I get it.
Have you been eating?

WILL: Of course I've been eating.

ARON: Every day?

WILL: Yes, every day. I get hungry, I eat.

ARON: Are you sure you always notice?

WILL: Yes.

ARON: If you didn't notice, would you know?

WILL: Yes I would know.

ARON: Because it's easy to miss those signals, when you've trained yourself not to care. Until it's too late.

(Beat)

WILL: Have you been eating?

ARON: I know that when a person doesn't eat or sleep, he loses track of time. Is that what unstuck means?

WILL: Have you been having time trouble? In your games? That's not how I taught you.

ARON: I'm playing okay.

WILL: If you were playing really well, I'd have heard about it.

ARON: If I were champion of the world, you might hear about it.

WILL: If an American were champion of the world again, it would transform the game. It would be the salvation of the game.

ARON: I hear you.

WILL: Don't shut me up.

ARON: I said, I hear you! I hear what you're telling me!

(WILL is silent.)

ARON: Dad. The not eating. Because work comes first. Is that what this is? But...you're retired, your children are grown, you're done working. You can eat now, you can rest. You have nothing more to do.

WILL: And why should such a person deserve to be fed?

ARON: Because a person is worth more than what he can do.

WILL: No. He is not.

(Beat)

ARON: Why aren't you sleeping?

WILL: Because my son has come home. And I never slept much.

ARON: You always said.

WILL: But lately, I don't know why, it's funny, you know what I started worrying about?

ARON: No, what.

WILL: It got in my head and I can't get it out, I have to get up, you ever do that, hoping I can leave it there, in the bed, and I'll stay out here till it decides to go bother somebody else. But I guess it followed me out here, 'cause I'm talking about it.

ARON: You're kind of talking about it.

WILL: Well, it's embarrassing. I keep thinking after I die...

ARON: Hey. That's not for long, long times yet.

WILL: No, I know.

ARON: You'll outlast us all.

WILL: Don't say—don't ever say that to me.

ARON: I didn't—

WILL: A son to a father. That is the last thing, the worst!

ARON: I hear you.

WILL: "I hear you," "I hear what you're saying," you say that a lot, it's a very noncommittal move, is that what I taught you? I keep thinking I'm going to die and you're going to turn into somebody else.

(ARON *is silent.*)

WILL: In the magazine I also saw there was a column with your name on the top.

ARON: Yes. That's my column, they gave me a column.

WILL: "Strategy Secrets of the Grandmasters?"

ARON: I know it's kind of... There's not a lot completely new to say about—

WILL: At the bottom of the column was the address of a website.

ARON: Yes.

WILL: You have a website.

ARON: I'm trying, yeah, game analysis, opening novelties—

WILL: I saw, I visited. It says you're taking private students.

ARON: Yeah. A few.

WILL: And there's a book.

ARON: Coming, yes, next month—

WILL: You wrote a book.

ARON: Collection of my best games, basically, with notes, you know, the usual kind of—

WILL: You're very busy.

ARON: Yes. That's. I haven't had a chance to come—

WILL: How do you have time to work on your game?

ARON: I do, I am, just in a different...I thought... winning, being champion again, I, the prize fund was pathetic, but the exposure, I was hoping, I could use the title, to piece together some kind of an, I don't know, a living. A life.

WILL: Sure. The years go by, you start to think, there's more to life than chess.

ARON: Yeah.

WILL: No. You're not missing a thing. People. You think they're happy? They're dead and their lives have no meaning. Believe me, I used to deal with them every

day. No principles. Not like you. You live by a code.
You're a warrior in the cause of logic and beauty.
Who can say that anymore? Yours is a fine, lone life.
A wandering knight, that's you.

(ARON is silent.)

WILL: Well? What's going to happen to all that, you
think?

ARON: When?

WILL: After.

ARON: After what?

WILL: After me.

(They watch each other.)

ARON: I hear what you're... Your parents died, what did
you do?

WILL: You don't—no, sure you don't remember, your
grandma, you were too young, and your grandpa died,
you were playing in a tournament, I didn't want it to
mess you up. And I was right. Where is it? *(Peering at
the trophies)* Regional Under-12 Champion, where is it?
There. See, you won.

ARON: I'm asking about you. He was your father.
We're talking about the deaths of fathers now.

WILL: Well, you have to understand, with me...
I was very angry at my father. So it was different.

(ARON is silent.)

WILL: And it was a different time, people expected
different things from a father. But that man...I got
nothing from him. Whatever I wanted to do, or to
make of myself. Nothing. Which from a father is worse
than nothing. So, I was really...I didn't even give him
a decent burial. Oh, and...we had no money, I had to
have him burned, I didn't want to give some vulture a

lot of money for some ornate casket or urn or
something.

ARON: *(A gesture to the shelves)* You could have used
one of these.

WILL: What? No, I could not, he never earned such
a thing in his life. But I swear I said just put him in
something simple. I didn't say cheap. They gave him
to me in a file box. His ashes. In a little sheet metal box
like you'd keep three-by-five cards in. With the lid
taped shut. They handed him to me at the cemetery
and pointed to the plot. So your mother and Hally and
I started walking across this big rolling swath of green.
He'd been a veteran, he was entitled. But—have you
ever been to a graveyard in Europe?

ARON: Whole place is a graveyard.

WILL: And the graveyards are like cities. Monuments.
Little buildings. Family homes. All these bitty houses
for the dead people to live. It's beautiful. An American
veteran's cemetery, it's like a filing system. White slabs,
green plots, green, white, green, white, to the horizon.

ARON: Like those roll-up vinyl chessboards.

WILL: Sure. They even give the plots a letter and
number, like the squares in chess notation. Little flags
stuck by some of the stones. Like the flags they put
on the table next to you at international tournaments.
No pieces, though. Just... Funny to think every square
on the board had its own little ghost, haunting it. And
I'm walking over this, holding this box. And the box...
coating of ash on it. Coming off on my fingers. Found
the right square on the grid. They'd dug a little hole.
I put him in. My finger caught on a metal spur on the
box. Cheap thing. Cut me.

ARON: Ow, I hate that.

WILL: Yeah, it was just a bad day all around. Put my finger in my mouth. And I'd touched those ashes.

ARON: God. What did it taste like?

WILL: What did it—tasted like chicken. Asshole.

ARON: Sorry.

WILL: "Hey, Dad, what did grandpa's ashes taste like?"

ARON: Sorry.

WILL: Tasted like ashes. You know that taste?

ARON: Yeah.

WILL: Yeah. Tasted like losing. Tasted just like losing.

(Beat)

ARON: But what did you do? After?

WILL: Oh... Did some thinking. Kept busy. Built this room.

(Beat)

ARON: Are you still mad at him?

WILL: Sure.

ARON: Even though he's dead to you?

WILL: Dead to *me*?

ARON: Dead, I mean.

WILL: Funny way to put it, he's dead to everybody, he's dead.

ARON: You like saying that?

WILL: It has its charm. So why are you here?

ARON: I told you. Don't you remember? Dad—

WILL: Oh, I remember some tub of shit about how I laid a little *non sequitor* on Hally, the phone went dead— did you call one of the neighbors? Did you call the cops? No, you dropped everything and came running in the middle of the Nationals. Sure. So what are you up to?

ARON: I told you.

WILL: You are here because you need something from me. And I wish you would once in your life admit it! And tell me what it is! So I can give it to you!

ARON: I told you something I want from you, I want something to eat! Have you given it to me?

WILL: I told you to help yourself! Make yourself at home!

ARON: This is not my home! I have a home! I am a grown man, I have a home and this is not it!

(They watch each other.)

WILL: All right. The game tomorrow. What can you tell me about him?

ARON: Oh, for—

WILL: What! Champions have coaches. Why do you want to go alone? What are you trying to prove?

ARON: Nothing!

WILL: Maybe that's the problem.

ARON: There's no problem, this is not why I'm...
I haven't seen the pairings for tomorrow, I've been traveling. That's why I want to go online, find out who it is and get to work on him.

WILL: Done.

ARON: Done?

WILL: I looked it up earlier this evening, all the pairings.

ARON: I thought you didn't know I was coming.

WILL: I do it all the time.

ARON: So who am I playing tomorrow?

WILL: You sure you want to know?

ARON: You're dying to tell me.

WILL: Guess. Come on.

(ARON *is silent*.)

WILL: It's that kid from Uzbekistan!

ARON: No it's not.

WILL: Yes, it is. Don't you read the tournament bulletins?

ARON: Just who I'm playing next, but with this one-day bye, the schedule changed, the pairings changed—how can he be—

WILL: You knew he was there, didn't you?

ARON: God damn it!

WILL: What happened to Mister I Need People Who Can Beat Me So I Get Better For the Good of the Game?

ARON: I hate losing! Losing is the death tax on winning. What is he doing here! What is a kid from Uzbekistan doing in the American National Championship?

WILL: He emigrated.

ARON: What? When?

WILL: A week ago. He lives here now.

ARON: What kind of idiot moves to America to play chess?

WILL: His whole family came. His village put up the money for them all to come to America.

ARON: Oh, great. So he's a story. I've got to play against a fucking story. The pride of Uzbekistan takes on the defending champion of the evil empire.

WILL: The evil empire? That was the Soviets. There's no evil empire.

ARON: I play against people from all over the world. Trust me.

WILL: They're trying to psyche you.

ARON: Maybe. But I know who they call the evil empire. I know what they think I'm the champion of.

WILL: They've got you tied in knots. Thank God you came to me. You've got to get another story in your head. You are esteemed. The world sends its best to test themselves against you. You teach them lessons and send them away, humbled and wiser. That sort of thing.

ARON: Dad. This is not... Okay. We're going to back up a few. Hally called me.

WILL: Said I was incoherent.

ARON: Said you guys were in the middle of a fight.

(WILL *is silent.*)

ARON: You have no memory of this? He says he shouted at you.

WILL: I don't remember your brother shouting at me.

ARON: Well, this is Hally. He might have thought he was shouting and you wouldn't necessarily know.

WILL: I might not necessarily hear.

ARON: Yeah. So he called me.

WILL: I admit it, he surprises me there.

ARON: He got back in touch a year ago, he heard I won the Nationals, called me up. Said it took having kids of his own to make him see.

WILL: Okay, see what?

ARON: That we were just children. That it wasn't my fault.

WILL: What wasn't your fault?

ARON: I don't know, his life?

WILL: What's wrong with his life, he has an easy life, far as I can tell, he's a lawyer, for God's sake.

ARON: He's a mediator, Dad.

WILL: Yeah, I know, that's just perfect.

ARON: Hey, how old are they now?

WILL: Hally's kids? Eight? Five?

ARON: Do they play, do you know?

(They watch each other.)

WILL: They're kids, of course they play.

ARON: You know what I mean.

WILL: Think about it, who's going to teach them, Hally?

ARON: You haven't taught them?

WILL: I want to! I keep offering to! First he said they were too young, now he changes the subject. Is your mother behind this, do you think?

ARON: Mom has not to my knowledge been part of this.

WILL: She's back there somewhere, you know she is. Why don't you teach them?

ARON: Because Hally said, the time we met and hashed things out, he said, one condition: never, ever teach them chess.

WILL: Why not? Why the hell not? To deprive them of all the—

ARON: Never going to happen.

WILL: I'm going to teach them. The next time they come, I'm going to sit them down, your old set is here, they're old enough, Kaylee's long since old enough, oh, this is going to be fun.

ARON: Dad. I don't—

WILL: I may not be able to give them much, maybe I've never been able to give anybody very much. But I sure know how to give somebody that. Oh, that'll be—

ARON: Dad? Don't.

WILL: What?

ARON: Don't teach the kids.

WILL: You're kidding.

ARON: I know it's hard.

WILL: If Hally feels like that, I mean if he feels that strongly, he can tell me so himself.

ARON: Dad. This is what he was shouting at you about.

(*Beat*)

WILL: So that whole... "Do they play, do you know?" That was a trap.

ARON: Little trap, yeah.

WILL: You would think it was some weird old-world religion or something, like I was sneaking them off to some cult ritual or some shrine or some—

ARON: Dad? Look a-fuckin'-round.

WILL: Some form of abuse of something.

(ARON *is silent.*)

WILL: This is wrong. There might be some real talent there.

ARON: They wouldn't enjoy it.

WILL: How would you—

ARON: They couldn't sit still for it, they never sit still, it's amazing.

WILL: How would you know?

ARON: I've seen them.

WILL: The kids? When? Where?

ARON: Fourth of July. Hally invited me.

WILL: You don't do holidays.

ARON: Hally invited me.

WILL: You never do holidays, holidays are for the open tournaments, they get a crowd of patzers, patzers on their chess vacations, you clean up at those.

ARON: Well, this year I went to Hally's. We ate food outside. It's a funny day, the Fourth of July, it's everything-upside-down day. They cook the food outside the house. The men cook. I was dressed completely wrong.

WILL: You wore the suit, didn't you.

ARON: It's a holiday. I dressed up.

WILL: It's the Fourth of July.

ARON: I forgot! Sneakers and shorts and t-shirts, I forgot there was a holiday where you dress worse than usual? I guess 'cause, what, it's a day about being free? The whole day was like that, just...just absurd.

WILL: Was your mother there?

ARON: Yeah.

WILL: She is behind this. I knew it.

ARON: Why would she care?

WILL: Oh, life is a long, long grudge match, my son. You don't know. And who's the players and who's the

pieces.... People like chess 'cause it's simple. So do you
see her?

ARON: No.

WILL: Do you?

ARON: What for? She abandoned me.

WILL: Abandoned you? Shared custody, you know that,
she got Hally, I got you.

ARON: Please. That is not shared. That is divided.

WILL: Same thing.

ARON: No, it's not.

WILL: You were supposed to see her weekends and
holidays.

ARON: But I don't do holidays, I've never done
holidays, or weekends, that's when I play. She should
have gotten me weekdays and you could have had the
weekends and holidays.

WILL: That would have been a disaster. Weekends
is when you play, but weekdays is when you work.
Weekdays are for preparation. She never could have
handled that.

ARON: Right. So she abandoned me.

WILL: She didn't abandon you. I'm the one she
abandoned. You were not abandoned. She left you
with me.

(They watch each other.)

WILL: Fine. I can't believe you felt you had to—and the
Nationals—fine. So I'm supposed to promise not to
teach my grandchildren—

ARON: Or their cousins.

WILL: Or their cousins! How to play chess.

ARON: That's right.

(WILL *is silent.*)

ARON: I know you need—everybody needs something to keep them...to keep them. Going, but... You just need to find something else. That's all.

WILL: Hm. You know what? No.

ARON: No?

WILL: That's right. No. This is stupid and I won't agree to it.

ARON: So I'm supposed to, what, persuade you or something?

WILL: You can try.

ARON: I don't know how to persuade people of things. I'm no good at that shit.

WILL: Well, then, that's—

ARON: I only know how to beat them and humiliate them.

WILL: What is that? A threat? Is that a threat?

ARON: Dad. Not at all. Of course not.

(*They watch each other.*)

WILL: This game tomorrow. You knew you were going to be playing this Uzbekistan kid, didn't you.

ARON: Sure, sooner or later—not tomorrow, I figured in the final, or...

(*Beat*)

WILL: You haven't faced something like this in a long time.

ARON: I am here to see how you are. I swear to you.

WILL: Sure, I know. And to tell me the thing about the grandkids.

ARON: I feel strongly about that, Dad.

WILL: Sure, okay. So you're leaving now?

(ARON *is silent.*)

WILL: Remember the last time you came here? Before the Nationals last year? You picked a big fight with me, about, what was it?

ARON: I was thinking about taking a money job.

WILL: You slammed out of here. And had the tournament of your life. So. It's good we're having a talk.

ARON: I need to be gone in the morning.

WILL: So you're staying.

ARON: Just tonight.

WILL: Good. Good. We'll share some ideas. Because— I know I don't really know that much, not technically— but that's the point of the game, isn't it? A couple of guys bring their ideas to the table, their stories about how things ought to go. And they see who's right. Right?

(ARON *is silent.* WILL *exits.*)

ARON: Okay. So. He trapped me back. And now he's going to... And I can... And then... (*He looks at the trophies all around him.*)

(*The lights fade.*)

Scene Two

(No one is in the room. Then WILL *enters, carrying an hardwood inlaid Drueke chessboard and a polished mahogany box.)*

WILL: Here we are. Aron? Aron? Where'd you go? Aron! *(Beat)* He was here. He was here. *(Crossing to the new trophy, touching it)* Aron?

ARON *(Off)* In a sec!

WILL: What are you doing? I'm setting up!

(No answer. WILL *wipes the table clean. He sets the chessboard on it, and gazes at it. He opens the box. It holds a Jaques of London boxwood and ebony chess set, in the classic Staunton pattern, tournament scale, four-inch Kings. Top of the line, over the top, the most expensive thing in the room. Worn from years of use.* WILL *picks one up. He polishes it on his robe.)*

*(*ARON *enters. He is wearing jeans that are too short for him and an old chess tournament souvenir t-shirt.)*

WILL: Where'd you go?

ARON: I'm working, I'm working, see? *(He sits. He pretzels himself into the posture of someone half his age. He watches the empty chessboard.)*

WILL: Why are you wearing those?

ARON: They're my clothes?

WILL: They still fit you.

ARON: You don't eat much, you don't grow much.

WILL: Why are you dressed like you're seventeen?

ARON: That's all that's here. It's fine. I don't need new clothes all the time.

WILL: What happened to your suit?

ARON: I'll need it for tomorrow. Some chess people wear the same clothes for days on end. I try not to do that.

WILL: You're up to something.

ARON: I'm working. You want me to work, let me work. Jeez.

WILL: Why don't you set it up?

ARON: I think quicker without a set.

WILL: Just set it up?

(Beat. ARON groans like a teenager and sets up the chess pieces.)

WILL: Look at that. All he is.

ARON: Everywhere I go.

WILL: Parceled out into sixteen pieces of wood.

ARON: Every board I look at, it's this board.

WILL: The house has a chess kid again.

ARON: How are you there, Dad?

WILL: A little unstuck.

ARON: Get some sleep.

WILL: I don't sleep much.

(ARON is setting up the set. WILL watches.)

WILL: What pieces do you have tomorrow?

ARON: Black.

WILL: You've looked up his games? 'Cause I could—

ARON: Done.

WILL: Checked his openings?

ARON: Done.

WILL: Endgames?

ARON: He likes the endgame, he likes to trade the Queens early and simplify down, he's most at home when there's almost nothing to work with.

WILL: So?

ARON: So, duh, I've got to keep it complicated, make him deal with a lot of options. Welcome to America, shithead. *(Re the chess set)* There. Happy?

WILL: Yeah.

(ARON looks at WILL.)

WILL: Yeah! Ha! Bad move, kiddo. Look at this. The Prodigy Strategizes Amid the Spoils of Victory. And you tell me I don't want to have this again with my grandchildren? Ha!

ARON: I told you, I'm no good at persuading people of things.

WILL: That's what you had me for.

ARON: Let me work. *(He moves pieces, alternating white and black, strikingly fast, and stares at the resulting position.)*

WILL: Remember the time—where was that—they were going to make you play under that flickering fluorescent—

ARON: You always could spot the weakness.

WILL: They had paired you against an opponent rated a hundred points above you, three times your age, the pairing was unfair! I was just leveling the playing field.

ARON: You leveled it. Screaming over my table— "That lamp is strobing on and off over my son's board!"

WILL: Tournament director's, "Sir, I'm trying to start the clocks!"

ARON: The guy I'm playing—

WILL: "It's fine, I'm fine, it's fine with me"—

ARON: Everybody's staring up from their boards, nobody's playing their game—

WILL: Because they'd rather watch me beating on this guy under this flickering, strobing—

ARON: Remember you leaned down and said, "When I give the signal, start faking a seizure?"

WILL: I did! God I was good!

ARON: The tournament director shouting, "Rules are rules!"

WILL: Right! "Rules are rules!"

ARON: The call of the chess player.

WILL: "Rules are rules!"

ARON: I'm trying to work up a spit if you need me to froth at the mouth—

WILL: The director's begging—"Can we move the table?"

ARON: "No!"

WILL: "Can we change rooms?"

ARON: "No! How can you ask my little boy to play with all these distractions!" You're standing there screaming about distractions!

WILL: Finally he figures life's too short—

ARON: "Distractions! Distractions!"

WILL: So now two custodians—

ARON: Trying to get a twenty-foot ladder—

WILL: And a light bulb—

ARON: Through two hundred chess sets!

WILL: "Coming through! Coming through!" Crash! Bang!

ARON: Guy I was playing—

WILL: "I'm fine! Really!"

ARON: He was a rat in a stress experiment. You cut his I Q in half.

WILL: He was ready to eat his own feet.

ARON: Well, the *coup de grace*, the lamp was fixed, the clocks were started, you slam your fist on the table—

WILL & ARON: "There! Now you can play!"

ARON: He blundered on move ten. Totally boring game.

WILL: You beat him. You won.

ARON: You beat him. That trophy should have your name on it. *(He picks up whatever pieces may have been scattered during the previous, and sets them back on the board in the opening position.)*

WILL: Great days, great days. Do they think—do you suppose they think you're bringing me back there with you? Wouldn't that be something? The hotel lobbies I've walked into, all over the world, and watched the chess people fall silent. Wouldn't that be something again.

ARON: Dad.

WILL: I know, I know.

ARON: A lifetime ban.

WILL: I know!

ARON: A lifetime ban.

WILL: I just—if I—

ARON: From all official chess events.

WILL: Yes! I've got it! The letter—you see it?

ARON: I see it.

WILL: I framed it!

ARON: I know.

WILL: With pride! That, there, that's my trophy!

(ARON *turns from* WILL *to look at the chessboard. He moves pieces fast, alternating white and black, in a standard sequence of game-opening moves.*)

WILL: What is that?

(ARON *moves the pieces with more deliberation as he reaches the limits of theory.*)

WILL: That's a great variation. They should name that variation after you.

(ARON *is silent.*)

WILL: How many times have you taken people out to that position and killed them?

ARON: Till John found the move that refutes my attack. Nobody plays it anymore. They all think it's unsound. (*He makes four more moves. He pauses and gazes at the board. The pieces are in a very sharp and theoretically unclear late-opening position.*)

WILL: You've got something, don't you.

ARON: A little thought. I've been saving it up.

WILL: What have you got? Show me.

ARON: I just like looking at it. Maybe today.
God, let him play this today.

WILL: You think he might?

ARON: Well. He'd have to be willing to play my signature opening, this whole sequence of moves, against me, the American champion.

WILL: But he's never played you before, maybe he doesn't know what openings you prefer.

ARON: He knows. I'd know. He's young, he's new, looking to make his name. What better way to do it? We've been there.

WILL: So you think he thinks he's the new fast draw in town—

ARON: And he thinks he knows my game better than I do. Or he wouldn't be here. I bet he's got an idea of his own, waiting to pull the pin. So we'll take each other all the way out to here, nineteen moves each. This is the edge of theoretical praxis.

WILL: And then he'll walk into it.

ARON: And then we'll see who's right, and who's an asshole in front of everyone.

WILL: But you found a new move.

ARON: Not just a move. A whole combination. A sacrifice. Blows the whole position apart. And no one's found it but me. No one's played it, anyway.

WILL: Show me.

ARON: You wouldn't get it.

WILL: This position? Sure I would.

ARON: Okay. Make yourself at home. You've seen all my games.

WILL: I haven't seen all your games.

ARON: You've read the moves.

WILL: Years since I've seen a real game.

ARON: Not my fault. Lifetime ban. So what happens now?

(They stare at the board.)

WILL: They still talk about me?

ARON: Sure. They still want to know your secret.
How do you set out to raise a grandmaster.

WILL: Yeah? What do you tell them?

ARON: I tell them my father calculated, when I was
four years old, how many things I would need to know.
Openings, tactics, strategic positions, endgames. About
a hundred thousand things.

WILL: I just did the math.

ARON: So every day, from age four, I learned a certain
number of things. So many before I ate breakfast,
so many before I ate lunch, before I ate dinner,
before I could go to sleep... Adjusting for difficulty
and increasing as I got older.

WILL: And that's all there is to it.

(Beat. ARON *looks up.)*

ARON: What?

WILL: Hm?

ARON: That last? What you said?

WILL: What you were saying, I said, that's all there
is to it. Planning, application, discipline. And a finite
number of things.

ARON: Hm. Hm.

WILL: You know, I'm getting up to speed here.

ARON: Yeah. Yeah. *(Re the position)* This is good.
This deserves a snack.

WILL: I need to shop.

ARON: That's okay.

*(*ARON *takes down a trophy, undoes the top.)*

WILL: What are you doing? What is that?

ARON: Peanuts, cereal. Chex Mix. That was the snack we had around, remember, your favorite snack? Chex Mix.

WILL: You hid food?

ARON: I lived on this. You never knew? You never took any of these apart, looked inside them?

WILL: That's disgusting, give me that, I'll wash it out.

(ARON *puts a handful in his mouth.*)

WILL: Stop that!

ARON: It's okay.

WILL: That's twenty-year-old cereal!

ARON: Twenty...five, or I mistake my vintage. Found a move yet? (*He crunches loudly.*)

WILL: I thought you were in here working.

ARON: I was. I hid this stuff to stay alive on.
Like a chipmunk.

WILL: You lied to me.

ARON: I was a kid sneaking food, calm down.

WILL: I was teaching you discipline. You ate, you slept. You didn't act hungry.

ARON: "Only a loser acts how he feels."

WILL: You worked through meals without noticing. You worked till the sun came up.

(ARON *swallows and eats some more.*)

WILL: Stop that!

ARON: Why, is this...distracting you?

WILL: Fine. Do what you want.

(WILL *stares at the board.* ARON *watches him, crunching loudly.*)

ARON: Well?

WILL: Is it...

ARON: No.

WILL: I didn't say anything!

ARON: I saw where your eyes were moving, that's not it. *(He swallows and eats some more.)*

WILL: That can't be edible.

ARON: It's edible. One thing you learn playing chess: a lot of things turn out to be edible. *(Re the board)* Well?

WILL: I'm just... Wait...

ARON: Okay, maybe. Then what?

WILL: I'm not doing anything!

ARON: Yeah, you are. Here, here, here, right? But then what?

WILL: How do you do that!

ARON: Keep looking. *(He swallows and eats some more.)*

WILL: You can't be getting any nourishment out of that.

ARON: Oh, I'm getting plenty of nourishment out of this.

WILL: You're going to make yourself sick.

ARON: Can't be sick. Got a game. Remember that? "How can you be hungry? You've got a game! How can you be tired?" I was so dumb. You know, if I'd just done what you said, if I'd eaten only when you said, and lived exactly like you wanted, I would, at some tournament, I would have passed out. Collapsed. It would have taken a few times. But you know they had their eye on us, all I had to do... If I'd showed up starving, they would have taken me away. And I didn't. I didn't. I dreamed, no, let's be honest, I hallucinated sometimes, I was a passed pawn, every tournament

was another square up the board, and me, little Mister
Pawn, if I got through everything, and reached the last
square, the promotion square, I would be scooped
away, right off the board, and become any piece,
something more powerful, a Queen or a Knight.
Lightheaded, it felt like that, I was lifting up, to be set
down somewhere else. But then I'd get scared, dizzy,
where would that other place be? What could I do
there? What good is a chess piece that isn't on a
chessboard, it's nothing. So I'd eat from these,
and keep going.

WILL: So all these have food in them?

ARON: No. Of course not. *(Strolling down the rows of
trophies)* There was one I used to piss in. Where is that?

WILL: Oh my God.

ARON: There we go.

WILL: The National Under-18 Championship Cup?
You pissed in it?

ARON: You got suspicious of all the time I was taking
in the bathroom, remember?

WILL: I knew you were just procrastinating in there!
One sip of water, oops, got to go! You weren't getting
anything done!

(Beat. ARON keeps crunching.)

WILL: Stop that now!

(WILL grabs at the trophy. ARON lets him take it.)

WILL: You were a prodigy! A phenomenon!

(They watch each other.)

ARON: Okay. Coach. Time's up. What's the right move
here?

(Beat)

WILL: How would I know.

ARON: Sorry, what?

WILL: I said, how would I know.

ARON: You mean you can't figure it out?

WILL: No!

ARON: It's right in front of you! You were so close!
Look! Six candidate moves that I can see—boom boom
boom boom boom boom—and branching off of those—
ba-bing ba-bing ba-bing, or on the other hand ba-bing
ba-bing... It's a beautiful position. The good moves
don't simplify the situation. A beautiful position is not
reducible to a finite number of things. It makes more
things possible. You have to look far into the future to
see what's right to do now. But if you do, you can push
back this little bit of the unknown by a few more steps.
A beautiful move shows every piece on the board what
it was put in its place to do. Harmony. Sense. Mutual
support. Of everything for everything. Beauty. You
know? Everything that isn't just who beats who. Come
on! Figure it out!

WILL: I can't!

ARON: Why not?

WILL: Because I'm not the fucking grandmaster, am I!

ARON: No. You are not. The fucking grandmaster. So.
Before you say something like "That's all there is to
it!"—

WILL: Oh, come on! That's—all I meant—that was a
remark! A little—

ARON: Dad? It's the little moves, unconsidered, off the
cuff, you didn't mean any big thing, right?

WILL: Right!

ARON: Blunders. Those moves we call blunders. *(Beat)* Dad, look. Hally isn't going to be bringing his kids here.

WILL: What? Oh, we'll find a way. The holidays, we always—

ARON: Dad. Hally won't be bringing his children to this house anymore.

(Beat)

WILL: Why would you say a thing like that?

ARON: Look at this room. Do you see Hally's name here anywhere? Do you see a trace of Hally here?

WILL: Whose fault is that?

ARON: Dad—

WILL: I'm asking you, whose fault is that? Mine or Hally's?

ARON: Dad. This is the kind of room where people ask that kind of question. Do you understand that? This room is all about who did better and who did worse. Hally's children shouldn't be here.

WILL: Well, good luck to Hally's children in America, because they're going to be walking into this room all their lives.

(ARON is silent.)

WILL: Fine. I can meet him halfway. More than halfway. He'll see. I'll come to them. It's better that way, there's only one of me, it's cheaper. I'll come to them.

ARON: Dad. Has he invited you?

(WILL is silent.)

ARON: You've always just announced you were coming. You assumed you were welcome. And he welcomed you.

(WILL *is silent.*)

ARON: Has he ever asked you to come to his home?

WILL: Of course he has. He has, of course he has.

(ARON *is silent.*)

WILL: Because of—what you were saying? Because of chess?

(ARON *is silent.*)

WILL: I don't understand.

(ARON *is silent.*)

WILL: Is this what he asked you to come here to tell me? And you've just been, what, been playing with me all this time?

ARON: No. This is one of the things I'm here to decide.

WILL: Well, it's not really up to you.

ARON: Yes, it is.

WILL: Maybe I'll drop by anyway. Yeah. Bring some presents for the kids. He's not going to bar the door. Not our Hally.

ARON: It'll be an uncomfortable scene.

(WILL *waits.*)

ARON: Of course you thrive on those.

WILL: Secret of our success.

ARON: No, Dad. The kids don't come here. You don't go there.

WILL: A lifetime ban, huh?

ARON: Yes.

WILL: Hally isn't a lifetime-banning sort of guy.

ARON: This isn't up to him.

WILL: Yeah, it is.

ARON: Do you want to see me again? Ever?

WILL: Is that your big threat?

(ARON *is silent.*)

WILL: You'll show up when you want something.
Like always.

ARON: You think, to talk to you, I need to show up
here? How many times have I had this conversation?

WILL: You don't have to tell me.

ARON: This is my set. This is the one I always see.
I have this conversation with you a lot, okay? I put
a lot of work into it.

WILL: Yeah, well, so do I.

ARON: Chess people, walking along, talking to
themselves, I don't do that. People think I am,
and I'm not, I don't talk to myself, I argue with you!

WILL: I sit here, like I'm sitting here now, every night—

ARON: You're sure? Lucky you. For all I know,
I could be in a hotel room somewhere, having this
conversation. I could be walking down the street on my
way to the playing hall, having this conversation. The
same one, again and again, did I have it already, could I
ever really have it, am I remembering, am I imagining—

WILL: And you start to feel a little unstuck. Yeah.
All night I've been thinking you're going to disappear.
If I stop picturing you for one moment. And I wouldn't
even notice, because I know what you're going to say,
I've got my strategy ready. I sit here, every night—

ARON: Oh can we for God's sake not make a
competition out of this? Can't we share anything?
Do we always have to divide it up?

WILL: Oh ho! And that, that is your mother talking.

ARON: No it is not.

WILL: To the life, what she would say.

ARON: Maybe it's just what anybody would say back to you. Maybe that's just what you do to everyone!

WILL: I want to know who's behind this. This is their revenge, don't you see that? On both of us.

ARON: Whose revenge? Whose?

WILL: I don't know! I lie there thinking—who is doing this to us? Whose fault is this?

ARON: And?

WILL: I think you're still being coached. Just not by me.

ARON: No, I am not.

WILL: Are you sure? Is there a girl in this again?

(Beat)

ARON: Cheap shot, Dad.

WILL: It's just—you talk about wanting a life, you've had a life—it wasn't—

ARON: All right, fair enough, I bring up your blunders, you bring up my blunders—

WILL: You were seventeen years old. The Champion of the United States of America. Who gets married at seventeen years old?

ARON: Somebody very tired and hungry.

(WILL *is silent.*)

ARON: She liked chess. A girl who liked chess. That's what I thought anyway.

WILL: But no?

ARON: Took me years to figure out. At first, we talked
about chess, all the time. But then I talked about chess
and she would talk about us. Finally I would talk about
chess and she wouldn't say anything. Nothing to offer.
Pissed me off.

WILL: Well, whose fault was that?

ARON: It turns out, if a woman comes up to you, and
she's asking you about chess, and she wants to talk
with you about chess, and she wants to learn from you
all about chess? She doesn't like chess.

WILL: No?

ARON: No, she likes you. I was so pissed off.

WILL: Yeah, well. I thought *I* could have a family and
the game.

ARON: But no?

WILL: Some can. I couldn't. So it came down to choice.
And there is no choice. One thing is better, one thing is
worse.

ARON: I never knew you were ever that serious about
your chess.

WILL: Not *my* chess.

ARON: So there I am. Seventeen years old. A freak show.

WILL: Seventeen, everybody's a freak show.

ARON: Seventeen years old. Divorced. Father banned
from the game. Champion to laughingstock in one year.
And here again, so dumb, I could have walked away,
just...I could have gone to college. And I couldn't do it.
I couldn't let them do it. No, I spend the next ten
years learning to play all over again. None of your
gamesmanship. Pure chess.

WILL: And to think you almost left for that money job.
And then you won! You won! You did it!

ARON: Yeah. To this day, so dumb. I'd always thought, I'll show them, I'll win again, and then I will walk away. But now, it isn't about winning. It's never about winning, except when I'm here.

WILL: You love to win.

ARON: Nah, I just hate like hell to lose. But you've got to win, or you don't get to play against the best, and if you don't play against the best, you can't really learn what they have to teach you. And you can't keep seeing deeper in.

(ARON *watches the chessboard.* WILL *watches* ARON.)

WILL: So. What is the right move?

ARON: No, no. The first person who sees me make this sacrifice, he's going to have to pay dear.

WILL: Asshole!

(WILL *swings a slap at* ARON's *head, but* ARON *leans just out of range and the blow misses.*)

ARON: Hey! This is how chess people learn! Somebody makes you feel like shit, but he shows you something. Now, I told you, the combination to look for is the one with the sacrifice in it. This is what the kids don't get, they just try to take each others' pieces, like whoever has the most stuff wins. But the masters, we're always looking for what we can give up to break the game open. Because your pieces don't matter. Right? Only victory matters. That's what takes the beauty prizes, when you sacrifice everything, and leave yourself just enough to win.

WILL: You are a great player.

ARON: Oh, I can see as deep as anyone in the world now. Except the best. I hate this game, I hate this fucking game.

(*They are silent for a while.*)

WILL: Aron, I swear to you, you could not have achieved what you have—

ARON: You know you can play tunes on these? *(Walking to one wall of trophies)* I worked it out one night. It's like a big xylophone. *(Using a small trophy, he starts tapping on the others.)*

WILL: You could not have achieved what you have if you did not love something here. It can't be done.

ARON: *(Singing along as he taps out a tune)* From the Halls of Montezuma to the shores of Tripoli,

WILL: Aron.

ARON: *(Singing and tapping)* We will fight our country's battles on the land and on the sea.

WILL: Aron.

ARON: *(Singing and pounding)*
We will fight to dum dee dum dee dum
And to dum dee dum dee deen
And we're proud to claim the title
Of United States Champeen.

WILL: I swear. If you have suffered, you have suffered out of love.

(Beat)

ARON: Why did Mom leave?

WILL: Ask her. Have you asked her?

ARON: Not as such.

WILL: You've seen her, though, right? Fourth of July?

ARON: Yeah.

WILL: You talked.

ARON: Not really.

WILL: So you're asking me. You're asking me why she left.

ARON: No.

WILL: You did. Back up a few. You did.

ARON: Never mind.

WILL: No, no. You've never asked me that before. It's novel. Did somebody suggest that you ask me that question?

ARON: No.

WILL: Look at me. Your mother, or Hally, or—

ARON: Why is it so hard for you to believe I'm here on my own?

WILL: Because you are full of this story about a poor sweet boy forced into competition by his mean old Dad. Who must be stopped before he strikes again. That's the gist of it, right?

ARON: Something like.

WILL: Nothing like. Nothing. You were a hellion! Anybody came close, whack! Smack! Your mother. You blacked her eye one time with a Matchbox car. She thought you hated her. Like raising a sea urchin, try to pick you up and ow ow ow! You could be a sweet kid, I'm not... But with this, I don't know, animal trapped inside.

ARON: This is weird. Why haven't I heard this before?

WILL: It's true! You came into this family like a panther or something. Something little and fierce. A wolverine. We tried everything. I play the piano a little, did you know that?

ARON: No.

WILL: You don't remember me showing you how to play the piano a little?

ARON: No.

WILL: You were all thumbs. The baby dance classes your mother took you to, remember those?

ARON: No.

WILL: You had two left feet. I taught you to throw a ball, you remember that?

ARON: I still can't throw a ball very well.

WILL: You threw like a girl.

ARON: What's your point?

WILL: My point is, from the age of four, you played chess like a man. A strong man. What you were asked to do—all you were ever asked to do—was to learn how to make the most of yourself. When did you ever get the idea that what I loved was chess?

ARON: But when did it get to be this life and death thing?

WILL: Gee, I don't know. When it took over my house? When it lost me one of my sons? When my wife left me over it?

ARON: I never asked for that.

WILL: You demanded it. You demanded it!

ARON: When! How!

WILL: By who you were! Just by being who you were! By seizing...you don't remember, why should you, your first breath your first steps a child doesn't remember, the parent remembers. When you learned chess. You seized it. You... "Play again, Dad! Play again! Play again!" We lay awake, your mother and I. What do we do? What is enough of a response to...who this is? Any

parent. We were...how it started, we were doing what
you do. And then...people will not take all the steps to
their logical conclusion. They are ground to a halt by
what's normal. And that's fine. But not in this case.
To see a child seize on a thing. Devour it. Devouring.
"More moves, Daddy! More traps, more tactics! More
people to play!" We kept trying to keep up! Time,
money, career, marriage, other children, having other
children, having any more children, did that never
register with you, you're the last, why that might be?
Your mother thought it might be nice to have one more.
Had always wanted a large family. I said, finally,
I mean, how many conversations was this, how many
years, I said, we have a large family. There he is. Oh,
and your big brother. Him too.

ARON: I never asked for this.

WILL: You weren't a bad kid. But your talent. Your
talent was a fucking animal. We threw everything in.
It wasn't your fault. Everything, trying to feed this...

ARON: Is that true? About me hitting everybody?

WILL: Why do you think I drove you and drove
you—drove us both—to all those places? Because
I was afraid of what you might do if I stopped.

ARON: Because I threw tantrums or something?

WILL: Rages. Beatings! And all this time, the chess
world thought... You think I liked walking into
tournaments and acting like an asshole? I was,
let's face it, a paper-pushing drone. What did I know
about how to get my way? But you know who I learned
from? You. You never let up! Everything I know about
gamesmanship, I learned from you when you were
three years old. But once you were in the circuit,
I didn't want you doing that, it would have broken
your focus. So I did it for you.

ARON: And chess, chess is what...it's my...

WILL: Medication.

ARON: Or my punishment or something.

WILL: It's a war game. A fine pastime for weak people who need to fight. Like the Law, come to think of it. Thanks to chess, everyone you saw, you could beat them and beat them, and nobody came up to say, "Sir, there's a problem with your son." No one saying, "We don't want him playing with our children anymore." On the contrary! They offered their children up to you! You beat them and beat them.

ARON: I helped those children. They didn't care about the game. I beat 'em so quick, the parents would take pity on them. Take 'em home, saying—oh, and they'd say it just loud enough for me to hear, "Well, he plays a very strong game, of course, but if you have to raise a child to be that kind of freak... Well, I'm just glad ours is normal. Let's go home, munchkin."

WILL: Oh, they made sure I heard them, too.

ARON: I set more little kids free that way.

WILL: *(Pointing to a trophy)* National Under-12 Champion. Nine years old.

ARON: Champion of the Children. Make way, make way.

WILL: Chess came along in the nick of time. Saved your life. Probably a few other lives along with. And then. And then. When it had turned you from this, this...

ARON: Sea urchin, wolverine... Monster, you can say it.

WILL: Into a grandmaster! Your mother. I'm here, she's sitting where you are—she goes, "Why can't we just raise him to be a regular person."

ARON: Really? She said that?

WILL: A regular person. An average person.

ARON: So somebody at some point actually said that.

WILL: And I go, "Why"—I mean—"why the hell would
we want to do that?" And she goes, "It might be easier
for him." I go, "What would?" She goes, "To find
somebody to love him." And I go, "Why do you think
somebody would be more likely to love a regular,
an average," quote unquote "person," and she goes,
"Well, honey, I love you."

ARON: Wo.

WILL: Can you imagine?

ARON: Ow. I can see why you've never told me that
one before. Ow, it burns.

WILL: All right now.

ARON: I can see why you'd spend your life nursing
a grudge against someone who nailed you like that.
"Well, honey, I love *you*." Go Mom.

WILL: Go Mom?

ARON: I just didn't think she had it in her.

WILL: She didn't. Not then. Finally it was too much for
her.

ARON: It was? I was.

(WILL *is silent.*)

ARON: So if chess was never that big a thing for you,
why teach it to the children? What's the point of that?

WILL: It's an excellent pastime for young and old alike.

ARON: But, but, really, all it is—it isn't even about chess
at all. Is it. You're just...

WILL: Planting the flag. In their turf. Yeah.

ARON: You don't even like them.

WILL: They're mine! Even if you hate something, it's hard to give it up. Isn't it? When it's all you've got?

(Beat)

ARON: Dad. The kids. They have no strategy. It's beautiful, they just...Fourth of July. Oh my God, running all over, soaking each other with water, jumping in the pool, out of the pool, running with fiery things in their hands...I'm sitting on the sofa in my suit, watching the cars go round and round on T V. Just quiet. A pack of kids go screaming through. Walker comes barreling into my knees, he grabs my hand, he goes, "You wanna play with us? Come on, come play with us."

WILL: Is this what's behind all this? You want little friends, little childhood friends, you want—

ARON: I'm telling you about your grandchildren! People are supposed to love to hear about their grandchildren! The kids weren't playing anything. They were just...playing! Like at one point one bunch of cousins took all the sofa cushions and dining room chairs and built this fort. And the other bunch of cousins got a bunch of pillows and stuffed animals. This was my team. And they were just going to all run in and attack this fort, but I said, I said if we send the littlest ones in first, like three toddlers, boom boom boom, then you guys slant in from the dining room and pile on, and then I'll charge in with the beanbag chair and wipe 'em out. We creamed 'em. I haven't had that much fun...

WILL: So they played the Sicilian Dragon Defense and you used a Yugoslav Attack.

ARON: What?

WILL: Black set up a fortress, right, on the kingside, and you, the white pieces, you sent a pawn storm up the

kingside, that's the toddlers, then a Bishop exchange
across the middle, slantways, and then you brought up
the heavy pieces, Queen and Rooks, that's you. Classic
attacking strategy. Way to go. You taught them chess.

ARON: No.

WILL: You taught them chess! Ha! Ha!! I'm proud of
you, son. You haven't made me this proud in years and
years.

WILL: I haven't—Dad. I just brought you the trophy—
I'm the Champion of the United States of America.

WILL: Oh please.

ARON: What.

WILL: Do I have to say this to you? You won the U S
Championship. And you're proud of that.

ARON: Shouldn't I be?

WILL: Oh please! While you were doing that, the cream
of international chess was in Linares, and nobody even
worried about the scheduling conflict because the
championship of the United States is not considered
by international chess to be a major tournament.
And you know that. And still you walk in here
bragging you're the American champion of something
not even America gives a shit about!

ARON: I can't help it if Americans don't care about
chess!

WILL: Of course you can! America doesn't care who
the American champion of chess is because America
doesn't care who the American champion of anything
is. America only cares who the world champion is.
Anything America cares about, we call the American
champion the world champion: baseball, basketball,
football. But anything where the rest of the world has
something to teach us, we do not want to know.

America cared about you when it looked like you might become the best in the world. But you're only the best in America, so nobody cares about you anymore. Except me, because God help me, I still believe you have it in you to be the champion of the world. But you will not make the commitment!

ARON: All the times—I told you—all the times I could have walked away—

WILL: But you didn't, because you knew I would know. You think I'm hungry and up nights because I'm ready to die? I'm afraid I'm going to die before you learn to be a winner! That's what is killing me! I am working, still working, trying to raise a winner!

(They watch each other.)

ARON: Okay. Okay. I was how old, I'd just won the States, or maybe the Regionals, I was eight. *(Looking around, pointing to a trophy)* That one. I was holding that one. And I said, "Daddy, I might not want to play so much anymore. Okay?" And you said: "Over. My. Dead. Body."

WILL: That didn't happen. I don't remember that.

ARON: "Over my dead body."

WILL: I would remember.

ARON: You said it more than once.

WILL: I didn't mean it.

ARON: Of course you didn't. You were younger than me now, you couldn't imagine your dead body. But I could. A child imagines the scariest things. You were saying I had the scariest thing in my power. Just by stopping. My chess kept death away.

WILL: So that's why you're here. To see how soon till you're free. *(Beat)* All my years. Devoted. And all you remember. A couple of offhand remarks.

ARON: Yeah. That's how it is, in this bitch of a game.
(He starts taking trophies off the shelves.)

WILL: What are you doing? What, this is your big threat
now, you're going to take your trophies and go? Is that
what you're going to do?

ARON: Let's see, this is... National Under-10
Championship. *(He unscrews the top of a trophy.
He overturns it. Out falls a pile of gray powder.)*

WILL: God, that stuff is rotten.

ARON: It's not food. *(Opening another)* Hally did hate
me, for a while. It was so clear who your favorite was.
Late at night, in our room, I was scared he'd hurt me
in my sleep, kill me even, so he'd have you to himself
again. So one night I told him about "Over My Dead
Body." He liked it. He had me tell it again. I told it a lot.
It was our ghost story. "Over My Dead Body." It got
to be a game we played, me and Hally, back and forth.
Like when Hally first heard about heart attacks. We lay
awake, so excited. Hally said a person can get so pissed
off he dies, right there. Pissed off to death. We thought
about that for a long time. We picked out music for
your funeral.

WILL: What are those?

ARON: Hally told me about cremation, after Grandpa.
It gave us a new idea. *(He pours out another pile of gray
powder.)*

WILL: Those are ashes?

ARON: You and I would come home from a
tournament, and you'd dance the trophy around, and
put it up here, and I'd watch Hally watching this, and
I'd whisper, tonight we'll put him in. It was our private
award ceremony, Hally's and mine.

WILL: These are me?

(ARON *silently pours.*)

WILL: How did you... Where did you get ashes?

ARON: Different things. One time, Hally had done a report for school, on some kind of birds, with all these pictures of birds in colored pencil, he'd gotten an A+ on it, he was so proud.

WILL: And he burned it. And put it in here to be me.

ARON: The first time, we were like—I don't know who started first—crying, kind of. We were scared at what we'd done. We didn't know what would happen next. Then we were laughing because how ridiculous was that. We hadn't done anything, nothing had happened.

WILL: But it had. You'd killed me.

ARON: We hadn't killed you. See, to me, "Over My Dead Body" meant I could kill you by stopping. But Hally said that what you meant was that you *were* a dead body. Because Hally remembered a time when we had a Dad who loved us. I was too young to remember. All I knew was, the man Hally was so sad about had gone away. In his place was this man who kept me locked up and starving and made me work and work and completely ignored Hally. And no one would admit that our Dad was gone. That he had been killed, somehow, by chess.

WILL: All the years. Under this roof. The hate.

ARON: Dad. No. This is just how we could live with you. The dead can't lay a finger on us. Whatever you were doing, it wasn't real. It was being done by a dead body.

WILL: He calls me every week.

ARON: Every Sunday, yeah. He makes his little offering. He's got to act like a good son, what else can he do?

There are things he likes to remember about you.
From before everything.

WILL: From before you!

(ARON *is silent.*)

WILL: All these? They have ashes in them? My ashes?

ARON: The ones that aren't food, or dried piss, are ashes.

WILL: Is this...is this really true?

ARON: Look for yourself.

WILL: I don't believe you.

(ARON *pours ashes out of trophy after trophy.*)

ARON: My marriage license. Divorce papers. We made
it you, and we burned it.

WILL: Your marriage license? Divorce—but—

ARON: The magazine with my picture on the cover.
(He picks up the trophy he brought with him.)

WILL: Don't.

ARON: Hally calls you, I bring these, and that is
supposed to keep you satisfied. Because Hally and
me, we're...we are what we are. But you can't have the
children. It's hard to tell you this, I'd hoped I wouldn't
ever have to, it's the kind of thing you don't want to
have to tell your parents. You hope if you wait long
enough, they'll figure it out for themselves. You're dead.

WILL: To you.

ARON: To me, to Hally, to Mom...when you're dead to
everybody, you're dead. *(He opens the trophy and pours
ashes out.)* So stop losing sleep over what I'll do after
you're gone! I buried you years ago and here I am.
Still in the game. All right? All right? Why do I have
to keep doing this?!?

(Beat)

WILL: No. No. I don't believe any of this. These aren't even ashes.

ARON: Yes, they are.

WILL: No. See. These. These are old food. Just old food. Looks like ashes, because, they're from so long ago. These aren't burned at all. This is just what time does. So. See? You can eat them. You can. *(Licking his fingers)* Mm. Mm. You're right. You could eat these. If you had to. So. Good try, though. Nice try.

ARON: Dad. Stop.

WILL: Is this why you never come here?

ARON: I come here all the time.

WILL: You're not even here now. You're playing tomorrow's game.

ARON: And when I'm playing, where am I?

WILL: Some, some hotel, some nothing place—

ARON: I'm here. Dad, I'm always here.

WILL: Fine! Yes! Great! You're always here! I hear you! You're always here, and I can never help you.

ARON: Help me what?

WILL: Help you win! What have I ever done in my life but try to help you win?

ARON: Every time I prepare for a game. Every time I'm tired and hungry, I go to this room. I keep thinking, one of these times you won't be here. But you always are.

WILL: I've been dead for years. Says you.

ARON: You will never be dead to me. You will outlast us all.

WILL: Good. Good! I told you these aren't ashes.
I'm not dead.

ARON: So you're going to stay alive then?

WILL: Damn right.

(Beat)

ARON: Good.

WILL: Good?

(ARON seizes WILL's head. Kisses his cheek. Holds him hard)

ARON: I better go. Got a game.

WILL: Glad you came?

ARON: It was worth it.

WILL: You're ready for it now?

(ARON pulls away, still holding WILL.)

ARON: Yeah, Dad. Yeah.

(ARON exits. WILL holds the trophy.)

WILL: My champion. My champion.

END OF PLAY

www.ingramcontent.com/pod-product-compliance
Lightning Source LLC
Chambersburg PA
CBHW052221090426
42741CB00010B/2634